Good Deeds with Ali

Once upon a time there were two brothers Rayan and Zachariah. As they were playing in the park Zach asked: Everyone is excited Ramadan is near but I don't understand why, do you know what it means ?

Rayan replied: Yes, we call it the Holy month of Ramadan for many reasons, it's the the ninth month of our Islamic lunar calendar. In which, we fast from dusk until dawn that means no food, or water until the Maghreb prayer is called. We do this for 29 to 30 days and it ends when the new moon is sighted prompting the start of Eid Al Fitr celebration.

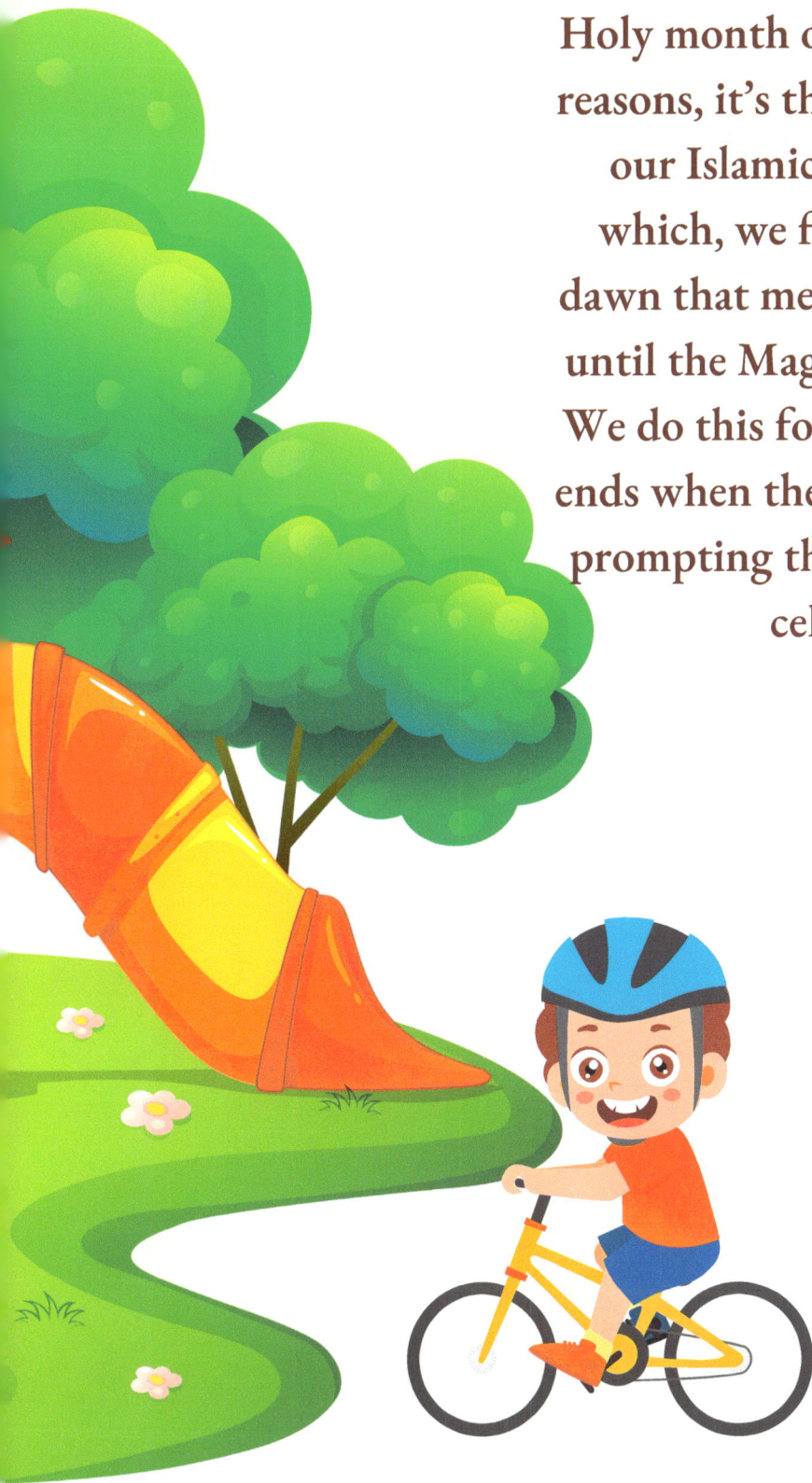

Zach replied: Wow, that sounds like a lot of hard work do I have to do it ?

Rayan replied: As you know Allah is most merciful. You are still young so you don't have to fast yet, but you can try for a couple of hours. Its very rewarding, you will feel amazing because you are following in the footsteps of our beloved prophet S.A.W. The elderly, the sick, pregnant women and travelers also are excused from fasting.

Zach smiled and nodded: I'm excited to go with daddy to the mosque, and eat all the amazing food and visit everyone like last year.

Rayan laughed and said: Oh yes me too ! Did you know that fasting is one of the 5 pillars of Islam like : Shahada, prayer (Salat), fasting (Swam), giving to charity (Zakat), and preforming Hajj to those who can.

It's also the month to get closer to Allah by preforming good deeds, but I don't know what good deeds we can do to gain hasanat, do you have any ideas?

Zach said as he smiled: I think I have an idea of who we can ask for help !

In the evening before bed
time, they decided to make
dua and ask Allah for help!

Dear Allah thank you for blessing us with the Holy month of Ramadan, and for giving us the chance to be better with fasting, praying and doing good deeds. Please help us find a way to do good deeds every day. Thank you, we love you Ameen.

The next morning
as the boys
were eating breakfast,
mommy gave
them a gift box.
They were very
excited to open it.
Zach was
jumping up and
down from
joy.

Zach: "Wohoo I wonder what it could be? "

Rayan Opened the box, a doll popped out with a note and a stack of flashcards. The note read: Hi, my name is Ali and I'm here to help guide you and show you how you can do small acts of kindness to get the most "Hasanat" good deeds during the blessed month of Ramadan. I'm so excited to be your friend, and make beautiful memories together.

Each day I will have a card for you that has an act of kindness " a good deed" and if you want, we can do it together; what do you say ?

Both boys shouted: Yes!

The next day they woke up they found Ali holding a box of cake mix, and next to him was a card that said : let's bake some sweets together and give it to our neighbors !

Ali, Rayan, Zach and mommy baked some delicious cupcakes and took them to their neighbor, who was delighted and very happy to have this sweet surprise.

In the days that followed, the boys and Ali enjoyed making lots of memories. They made a Sadaqah jar and donated the money at the end of Ramadan to the Mosque.

They invited their family over for Iftar.

They donated some of their old clothes and toys to charity.

They planted a tree in their grandma's yard.

They Prayed in the mosque, and made Dua for those they lost

And much more ...

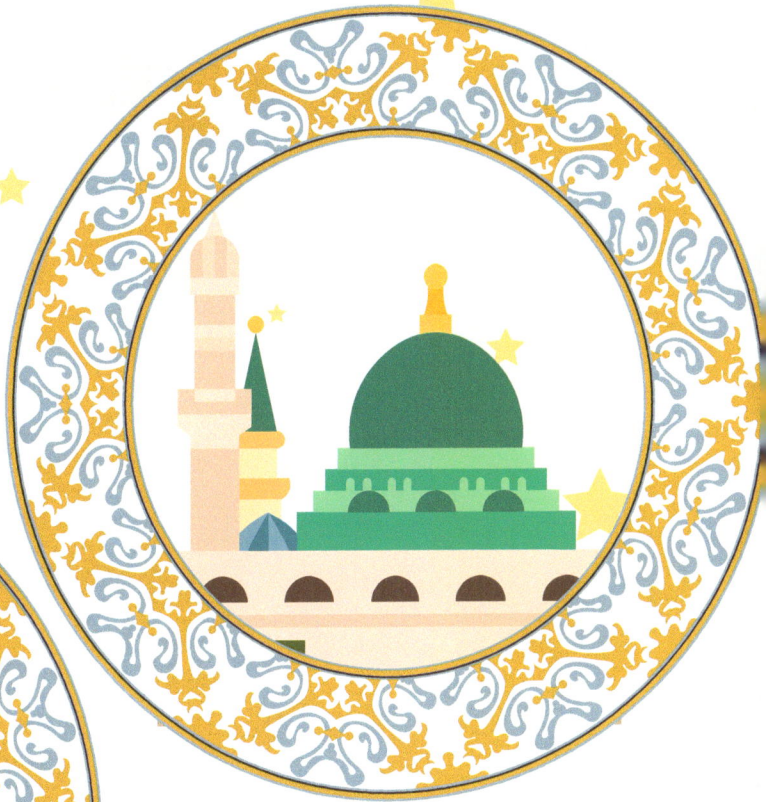

As Ramadan came to an end and Eid day is here, mommy surprised the boys and sewed an Eid outfit for Ali. Zach and Rayan were delighted. They laughed and expressed their happiness at all the good deeds they made this month, and how excited they are to do more during the year. They hugged Ali and made dua to Allah to thank him for all that he has given them in this life, and for giving them a special new friend " Ali".

During this coming month of Ramadan Rayan and Zachariah want to share Ali with you and your family to create wonderful memories like they did, and gain as many hasanat as you can. In the next pages you will find the flashcards the boys used to create these wonderful moments. Whether you purchased the book and Ali the toy bundle, or you're just enjoying reading this book, we hope you enjoyed reading it as much as we did making it for you.

We hope you have a blessed month of Ramadan and have a wonderful Eid.

1

2

3

4

5

6

Help set the
table for Iftar.

Smile at everyone
you see today.

Make a Sadaqah Jar.

Help clean the
table
after Iftar..

Donate a Toy to
charity, or to
someone who
doesn't have it. For
example: a hospital.

Donate a meal to
someone in need.
For example: buy a
meal
for a homeless man.

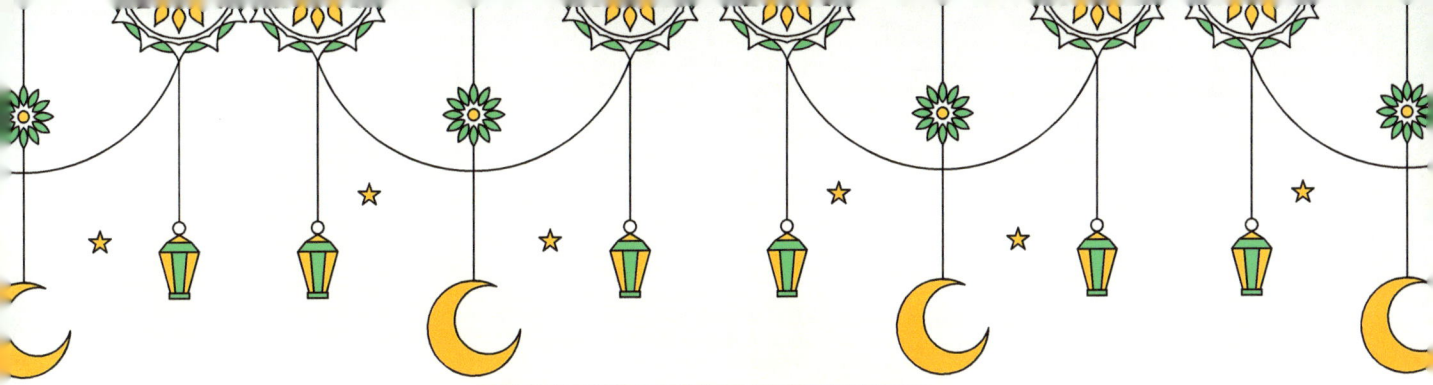

7

8

9

10

11

12

Help with household Chores.

Collect canned food to donate to a food bank.

Phone a family member for a chat.

Leave water out for the birds.

Write, or draw a thank you note to someone you love.

Plant a flower, or a tree.

13

14

15

16

17

18

Do something nice for a family member

Invite someone for Iftar.

Try to pray all five prayers on time.

Make a dua for a loved one you lost

Try to pray an extra two rakaat today

Donate some clothes to charity.

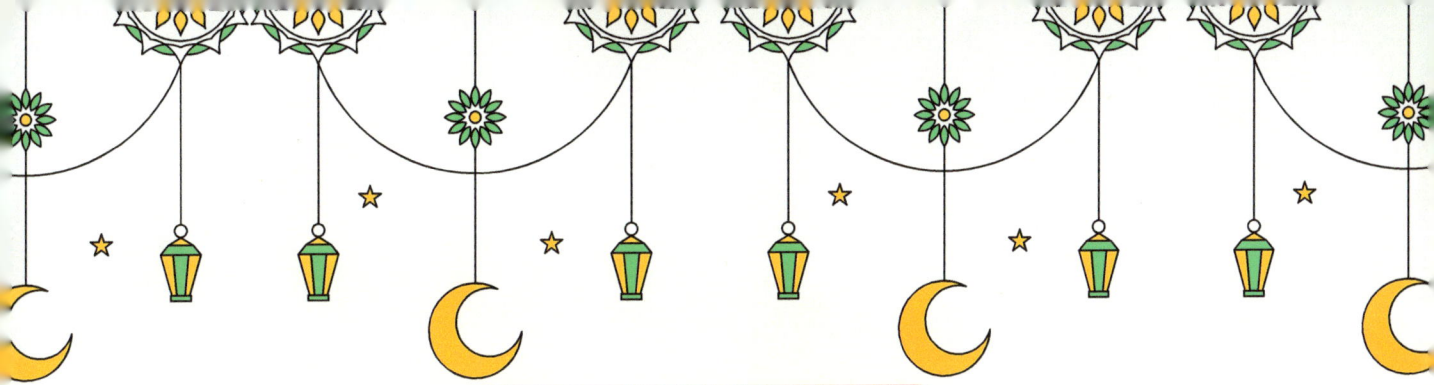

19

20

21

22

23

24

Make a Dua to
Thank Allah
for all we have.

Recite the
Quran.

Learn a new sunnah
of our Prophet
may peace be
upon him.

Make food,
or sweets
for your
neighbor.

compliment as many
people as you can while
greeting them with
" Al Salamo Aliekom"

Say Tasbih.

25

26

27

28

29

30

Learn a new Surah.

Try to pray one prayer at the masjid today.

Learn about laylat alkadr, and make a dua for your family.

Decorate your house for Eid.

Make Eid sweets or crafts for your loved ones.

Donate the money you collected in the Sadaqah Jar to someone in need, or to the donation box at the mosque

Glossary

Quran: The holy book of Islam.

Surah: is the equivalent of "chapter" in the Qur'an. There are 114 surahs in the Quran, each divided into ayats.

Dua: is a prayer of invocation, supplication or request, even asking help or assistance from Allah.

Tasbih: is a form of dhikr that involves the glorification of Allah in Islam by saying: "Subhan Allah"

Salat: the prayer of Muslims, performed five times daily

Masjid: The Arabic word for mosque

Hasanat: Good deeds, kind acts.

www.ingramcontent.com/pod-product-compliance
Lightning Source LLC
LaVergne TN
LVHW072130070426
835513LV00002B/55